MY JOURNAL

LOVE IN A BIG WORLD™

HELLO MY NAME IS

Love In A Big World
My Journal Grade 7

Copyright ©2021 BlueWonder Creative, LLC

All rights reserved.

No part of this work may be reproduced or transmitted in any form or by any means, electronic or mechanical, including photocopying and recording, or by any information storage or retrieval system, except as may be expressly permitted by the 1976 Copyright Act or in writing by the publisher.

Requests for permission should be addressed to Love In A Big World, PO Box 120364, Nashville, TN. 37212 1-800-843-4952, or e-mailed to info@loveinabigworld.org

Quotation References

Betz, Adrienne. *Scholastic Treasury of Quotations for Children.* New York: Scholastic, 1998

Author/Creator: Tamara Fyke
Community Edition
My Journal for Grade 7
Print Edition   9781737650645 frMANUFACTURED IN THE UNITED STATES OF AMERICA

ARE YOU READY TO START JOURNALING?

Once you've gathered crayons, markers, or pencils...

1. Quiet yourself.

Take three deep breaths. Count to five in your head as you inhale, and count to five in your head again as you exhale.

2. Reflect.

Think about what you've been learning and how it affects what you do and say. Listen to your heart.

3. Express yourself.

Color, write, and draw what you are thinking and feeling. There are no right or wrong answers. Be creative!

HEROES

CHOICE

THE OPPORTUNITY AND POWER TO MAKE DECISIONS

Choice

You have brains in your head. You have feet in your shoes. You can steer yourself any direction you choose. —Oh, The Places You'll Go! by Dr. Seuss (1904–1991)

Decisions are not always easy. Write about a time you had to make a difficult decision.

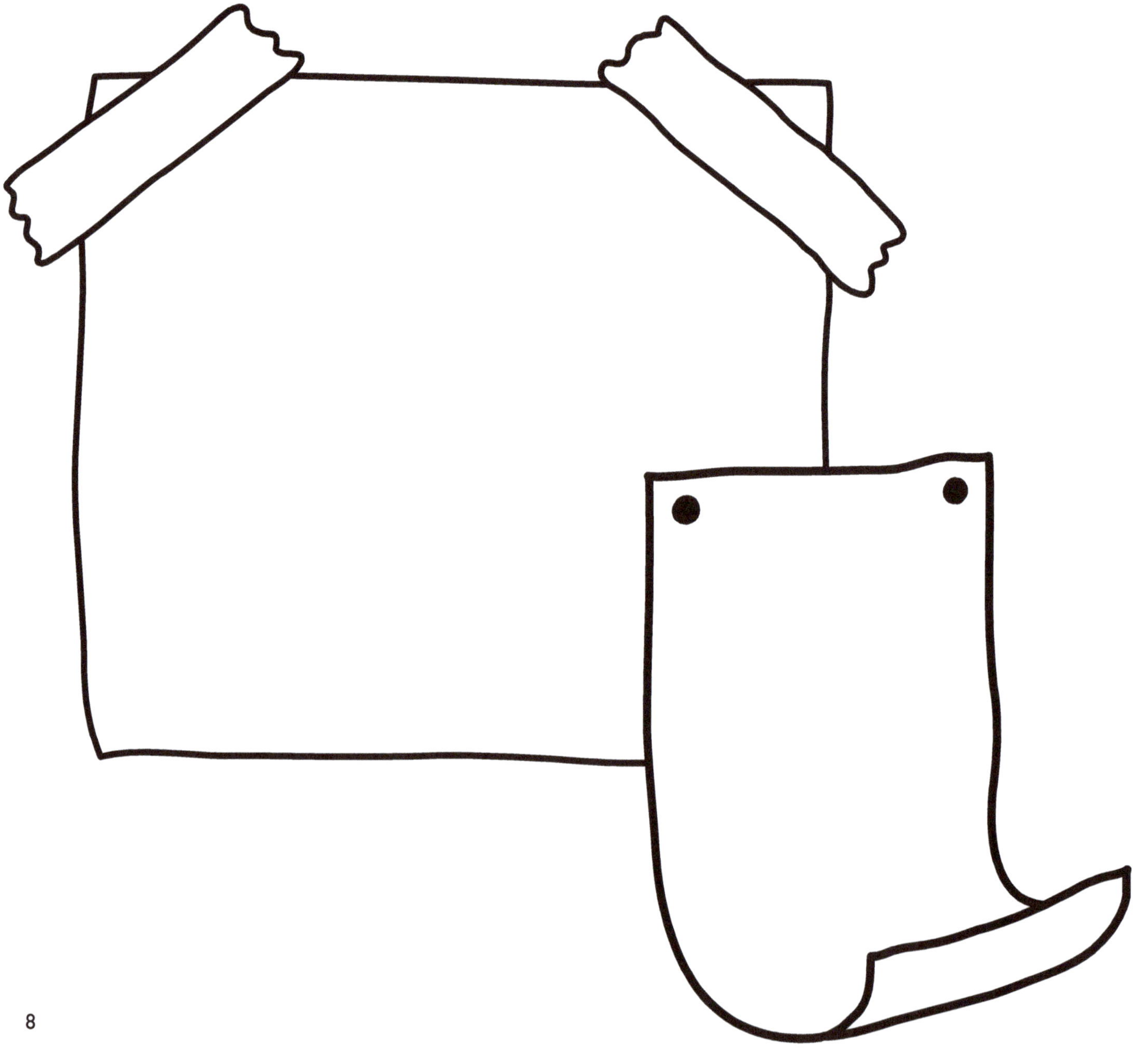

Heroes

COURAGE

STANDING UP FOR WHAT IS RIGHT; FACING YOUR FEARS

Courage

You gain strength, courage and confidence by every experience in which you stop to look fear directly in the face.
—Eleanor Roosevelt (1884–1962)

Write about an experience when you stood up for what was right and/or when you faced your fears about something specific.

HEROES

HONESTY

SPEAKING AND ACTING TRUTHFULLY; LIVING THE TRUTH

Honesty

Honesty is the best policy. —Miguel de Cervantes (1547–1616)

YOUR BIG WORLD

When were you honest in a difficult situation?

HEROES

KINDNESS

TREATING OTHERS THE WAY YOU WANT TO BE TREATED

Kindness

Shall we make a new rule of life . . . always try to be a little kinder than is necessary? —J.M. Barrie (1860–1937)

YOUR BIG WORLD

How can being kind to others lead to peace between groups?

Heroes

RESPONSIBILITY

TAKING CHARGE OF YOUR OWN WORDS AND ACTIONS

Responsibility

The time is always ripe for doing right. —Martin Luther King Jr. (1929–1968)

YOUR BIG WORLD

Is it easier to accept responsibility for something that turns out well or for something that fails? Why?

HEROES

SELF-CONTROL

MANAGING YOUR FEELINGS, ATTITUDES, AND ACTIONS

Self-Control

If your head tells you one thing and your heart tells you another, before you do anything, you should first decide whether you have a better head or a better heart.
—Marilyn vos Savant (b. 1946)

Share a time when you displayed significant self-control.

HEROES

GRATITUDE

BEING **THANKFUL** FOR WHAT YOU HAVE AND WHAT OTHERS **DO FOR YOU** OR **GIVE TO YOU**

Gratitude

Reflect upon your present blessings, of which every man has plenty; not on your past misfortunes, of which all men have some. —Charles Dickens (1812–1870)

YOUR BIG WORLD

For whom are you most grateful and why?

HEROES

SELF-AWARENESS

KNOWING YOUR STRENGTHS AND WEAKNESSES; BEING ABLE TO KNOW AND UNDERSTAND HOW YOU FEEL

Self-Awareness

Deal with yourself as an individual worthy of respect, and make everyone else deal with you the same way.
—Nikki Giovanni (b. 1943)

What is one thing about you that you feel is important for people to know?

Heroes

HUMILITY
not thinking too MUCH or too LITTLE of yourself

Humility

Do not measure another person's coat by how well it fits your body. —Malay Proverb

YOUR BIG WORLD

When you disagree with someone, are you willing to look at the big picture and give up your preferences? Why or why not?

HEROES

MODERATION

KEEPING A BALANCE; AVOIDING EXTREMES

Moderation

All the world is birthday cake, so take a piece, but not too much. —George Harrison (1943–2001)

YOUR BIG WORLD

Describe the difference between needs and wants.

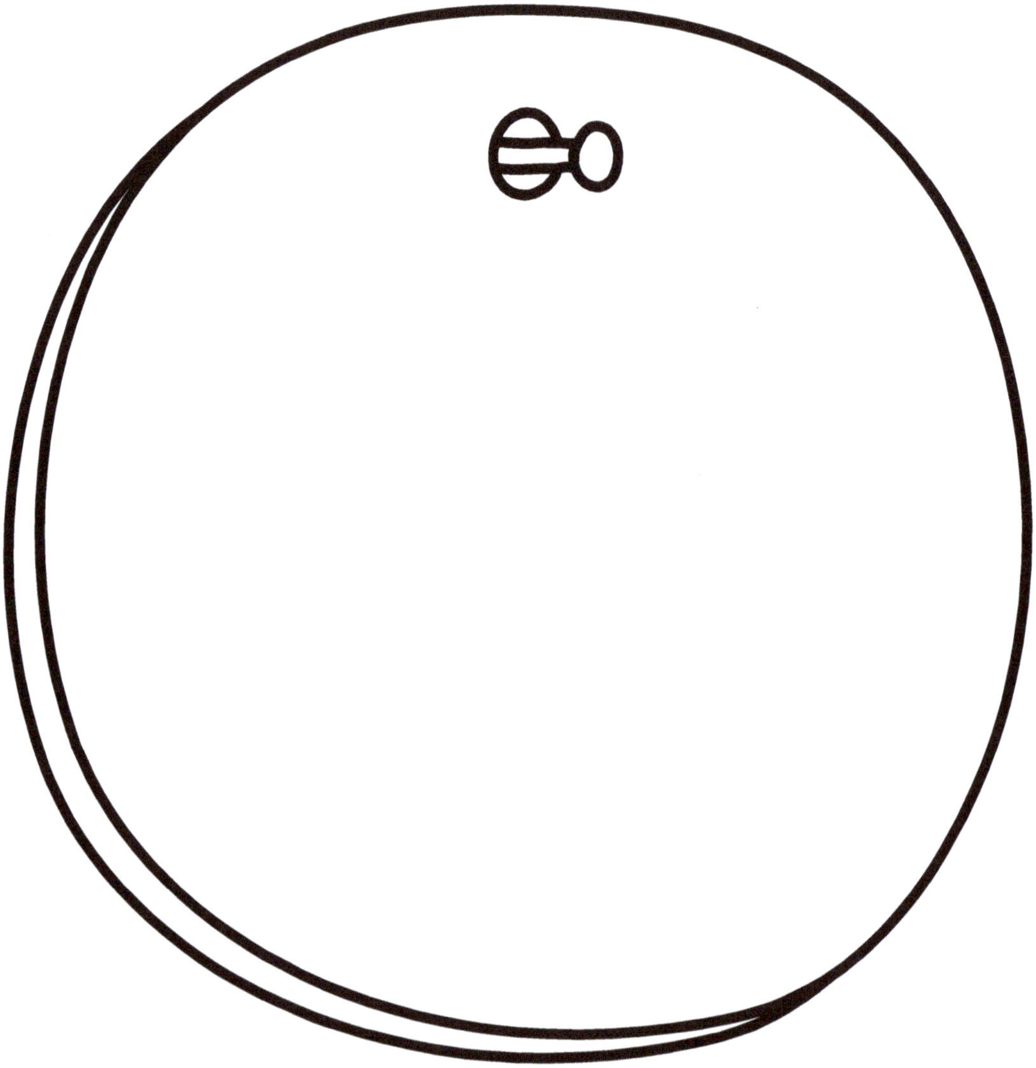

HEROES

PATIENCE

WAITING WITHOUT COMPLAINING: ACCEPTING PAIN OR CHALLENGES WITHOUT COMPLAINT

Patience

Rivers know this: there is no hurry. We shall get there some day. —Winnie-the-Pooh by A.A. Milne (1882–1956)

When have you had to be extremely patient?

HEROES

ORGANIZATION

KEEPING THINGS IN ORDER; HAVING A PLAN OF ACTION

Organization

An idea can only become a reality once it is broken down into organized, actionable elements. —Making Ideas Happen: Overcoming the Obstacles Between Vision and Reality by Scott Belsky (b. 1980)

YOUR BIG WORLD!

Why is it necessary to have action steps and organization to reach a goal?

HEROES

PURPOSE

DETERMINATION; SETTING GOALS; FINDING A REASON FOR BEING

Purpose

I am only one, But still I am one. I cannot do everything, But still I can do something: And because I cannot do everything I will not refuse to do the something that I can do. —Edward Everett Hall (1822–1909)

What talent or interest do you have right now that can better the lives of your family, friends, or neighborhood?

Heroes

CREATIVITY

THINKING OF NEW IDEAS: DREAMING OF WHAT COULD BE

Creativity

A person who has no imagination has no wings.
– Muhammad Ali (1942- 2016)

YOUR BIG WORLD

If you play a musical instrument, what do you like about it? What is challenging about it? If you do not play a musical instrument, which one do you wish you did and why?

HEROES

PERSEVERANCE

STICKING TO IT; NOT GIVING UP

Perseverance

Never give in, never give in, never, never, never, never—in nothing great or small, large or petty—never give in except to convictions of honor and good sense. —Winston Churchill (1874–1965)

YOUR BIG WORLD

Set a goal to complete by the end of this school year. Describe your goal and the steps to reach it.

Heroes

DEPENDABILITY

BEING ABLE TO BE COUNTED ON

Dependability

Dependability is that quality of sureness which makes folks know that the task assigned will be accomplished, that the promise made will be kept, a golden quality. . . . —Clarissa A. Beesley (1878–1974)

Why is it important to be dependable?

Heroes

RESPECT
Valuing yourself and others

Respect

A child who is allowed to be disrespectful to his parents will not have true respect for anyone. —Billy Graham (b. 1918)

YOUR BIG WORLD

What would you do if you saw a child mistreated in your neighborhood?

HEROES

FAIRNESS

TREATING EVERY PERSON THE SAME; PLAYING BY THE RULES

Fairness

When you've… walked through that doorway of opportunity, you do not slam it shut behind you. You reach back, and you give other folks the same chances that helped you succeed.
—Michelle Obama (b. 1964)

How do you feel when you play by the rules but you would prefer not to? Why is playing by the rules the best action?

HEROES

COURTESY

THINKING OF OTHERS FIRST; MINDING YOUR MANNERS

Courtesy

Children act in the village as they have learned at home.
—Swedish Proverb

How would you feel if your brother or sister was extremely rude to you in front of your friends at school?

CARING

Showing concern for the well-being of others; taking the time to let others know they are important

Caring

A smile is the light in your window that tells others that there is a caring, sharing person inside. —Denis Waitley (b. 1933)

YOUR BIG WORLD

After you graduate, what is your next step to continue learning?

Heroes

GENEROSITY

GIVING AND SHARING WITH OTHERS

Generosity

If you have much, give of your wealth. If you have little, give of your heart. —Arab Proverb

YOUR BIG WORLD

What is your most prized possession? If you were to give it away, whom would you give it to? Why would you give it to that person? How would this possession help him or her?

HEROES

COOPERATION

WORKING WITH OTHERS AS A TEAM

Cooperation

I have noticed that when chickens quit quarreling over their food they often find that there is enough for all of them. I wonder if it might not be the same way with the human race.
—Don Marquis (1878–1937)

Identify an individual or group that you want to help.
Why do you want to assist this individual or group?
What do you hope to accomplish together?

HEROES

FORGIVENESS

PUTTING ANOTHER'S WRONGS BEHIND; LETTING GO OF ANGER BECAUSE OF A WRONG

Forgiveness

Forgiveness is me giving up my right to hurt you for hurting me.
—Anonymous

Write about your day and identify if there is anyone whom you need to forgive for something he or she did that hurt your feelings.

HEROES

LOVE IN A BIG WORLD

BEING CHANGED BY LOVE: MAKING A POSITIVE DIFFERENCE BY CHOOSING TO LOVE

Love In A Big World

Never doubt that a small group of thoughtful, committed citizens can change the world. Indeed, it's the only thing that ever has. —Margaret Mead (1901–1978)

YOUR BIG WORLD

Do you think taking a stance of nonviolence can work in all situations? If so, why? If not, why not?